S0-BNG-196

COLORS DE LA RUNWAY

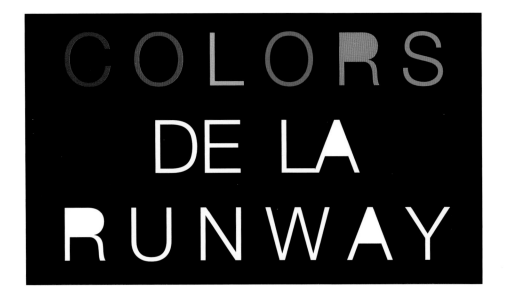

COLORS DE LA RUNWAY

BY CLARENCE RUTH

4880 Lower Valley Road • Atglen, PA 19310

RED

(rouge)

ORANGE

(orange)

YELLOW

(jaune)

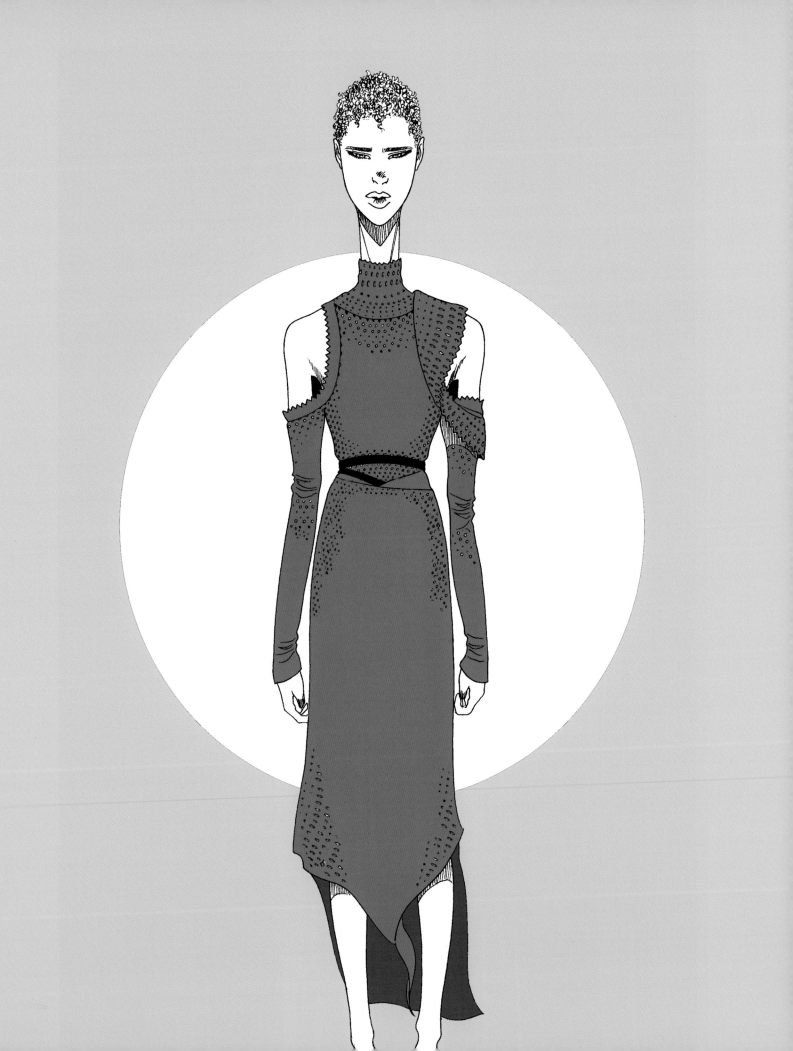

GREEN

(vert)

MULTI
COLORS

(multicolores)

LIGHT BLUE

(bleu clair)

Ready to Write a Book?

Our authors are as passionate as we are about providing new and intriguing perspectives on a variety of topics, both niche and general. If you have a fresh idea, we would love to hear from you, as we are continually seeking new authors and their work. Visit our website to view our complete list of titles and our current catalogs. Please visit our Author Resource Center on our website for submission guidelines, and contact us at proposals@schifferbooks.com or write to the address below, to the attention of Acquisitions.

⊗ Schiffer Publishing Ltd.

A family-owned, independent publisher since 1974, Schiffer has published thousands of titles on the diverse subjects that fuel our readers' passions. Explore our list of more than 5,000 titles in the following categories:

ART, DESIGN & ANTIQUES

Fine Art | Fashion | Architecture | Interior Design | Landscape | Decorative Arts | Pop Culture | Collectibles | Art History | Graffiti & Street Art | Photography | Pinup | Sculpture | Body Art & Tattoo | Antique Clocks | Watches | Graphic Design | Contemporary Craft | Illustration | Folk Art | Jewelry | Fabric Reference

MILITARY

Aviation | Naval | Ground Forces | American Civil War | Militaria | Modeling & Collectible Figures | Pinup | Transportation | World War I & II | Uniforms & Clothing | Biographies & Memoirs | Unit Histories | Emblems & Patches | Weapons & Artillery

CRAFT

Arts & Crafts | Fiber Arts & Wearable | Woodworking | Quilts | Gourding | Craft Techniques | Leathercraft | Carving | Boat Building | Knife Making | Printmaking | Weaving | How-to Projects | Tools | Calligraphy

TRADE

Lifestyle | Natural Sciences | History | Children's | Regional | Cookbooks | Entertaining | Guide Books | Wildlife | Tourism | Pets | Puzzles & Games | Movies | Business & Legal | Paranormal | UFOs | Cryptozoology | Vampires | Ghosts

MIND BODY SPIRIT

Divination | Meditation | Astrology | Numerology & Palmistry | Psychic Skills | Channeled Material | Metaphysics | Spirituality | Health & Lifestyle | Tarot & Oracles | Crystals | Wicca | Paganism | Self Improvement

MARITIME

Professional Maritime Instruction | Seamanship | Navigation | First Aid/Emergency | Maritime History | The Chesapeake | Antiques & Collectibles | Children's | Crafts | Natural Sciences | Hunting & Fishing | Cooking | Shipping | Sailing | Travel | Navigation

SCHIFFER PUBLISHING, LTD.
4880 Lower Valley Road, Atglen, PA 19310
Phone: 610-593-1777
E-mail: Info@schifferbooks.com
Printed in China

www.schifferbooks.co

BLUE

(bleu)

NAVY

(marine)

BURGUNDY

(bourgogne)

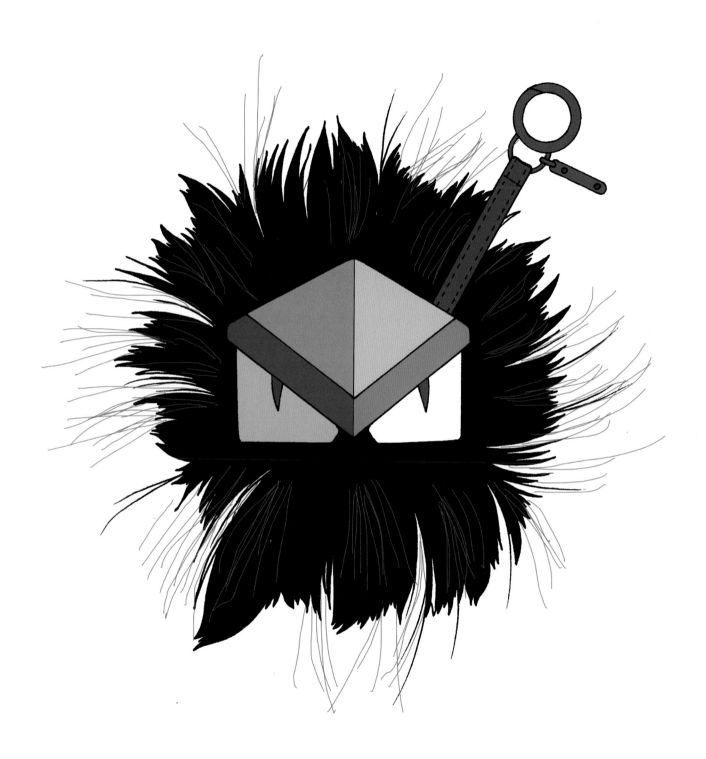

PURPLE

(violet)

PINK

(rose)

LIGHT
PINK

(rose clair)

BEIGE

(beige)

BROWN

(marron)

ARMY GREEN

(armée verte)

BLACK

(noir)

WHITE

(blanc)

GREY

(gris)

STRIPES

(rayures)

POLKA DOTS

DOTS

(À pois)

Edited by Kim Grandizio
Designed by Clarence Ruth
Type set in GeoSlab703/Helvetica

ISBN: 978-0-7643-5683-4
Printed in China

Published by Schiffer Publishing, Ltd.
4880 Lower Valley Road
Atglen, PA 19310
Phone: (610) 593-1777; Fax: (610) 593-2002
E-mail: Info@schifferbooks.com
Web: www.schifferbooks.com

For our complete selection of fine books on this and related subjects, please visit our website at www.schifferbooks.com. You may also write for a free catalog.

Schiffer Publishing's titles are available at special discounts for bulk purchases for sales promotions or premiums. Special editions, including personalized covers, corporate imprints, and excerpts, can be created in large quantities for special needs. For more information, contact the publisher.

We are always looking for people to write books on new and related subjects. If you have an idea for a book, please contact us at proposals@schifferbooks.com.

This work is not endorsed, approved, or affiliated with any of the designers featured in it.

CREDITS

Red
Pages: 4-5
Brand: Christopher Kane
Season: Autumn/Winter 2015
Creative Director: Christopher Kane
London Fashion Week

Orange
Pages: 6-7
Brand: Prada
Season: Spring/Summer 2017
Creative Director: Miuccia Prada
Milan Fashion Week

Yellow
Pages: 8-9
Brand: J. JS Lee
Season: Autumn/Winter 2016
Creative Director: Jackie Lee
London Fashion Week

Green
Pages: 10-11
Brand: Proenza Schouler
Season: Spring/Summer 2016
Creative Director: Lazaro Hernandez, Jack McCollouh
New York Fashion Week

Multi Colors
Pages: 12-13
Brand: Prada
Season: Autumn/Winter 2014
Creative Director: Miuccia Prada
Milan Fashion Week

Light Blue
Pages: 14-15
Brand: Hermes
Season: Autumn/Winter 2015
Creative Director: Nedege Vanhee-Cybulski
Paris Fashion Week

Blue
Pages: 16-17
Brand: Balenciaga
Season: Spring/Summer 2017
Creative Director: Demna Gvsalia
Paris Fashion Week

Navy
Pages: 18-19
Brand: Thom Browne
Season: Spring/Summer 2018
Creative Director: Thom Browne
Paris Fashion Week

Burgundy
Pages: 20-21
Brand: Fendi
Season: Autumn/Winter 2016
Creative Director: Karl Lagerfeld
Milan Fashion Week

Purple
Pages: 22-23
Brand: Loewe
Season: Autumn/Winter 2016
Creative Director: J.W Anderson
Paris Fashion Week

Pink
Pages: 24-25
Brand: 3.1 Phillip Lim
Season: Autumn/Winter 2016
Creative Director: Phillip Lim
New York Fashion Week

Light Pink
Pages: 26-27
Brand: Thom Browne
Season: Autumn/Winter 2012
Creative Director: Thom Browne
Paris Fashion Week

Beige
Pages: 28-29
Brand: Balencaga
Season: Autumn/Winter 2016
Creative Director: Demna Gvasalia
Paris Fashion Week

Brown
Pages: 30-31
Brand: Marni
Season: Autumn/Winter 2016
Creative Director: Consuelo Castiglioni
Milan Fashion Week

Army Green
Pages: 32-33
Brand: Marni
Season: Spring/Summer 2017
Creative Director: Consuelo Castiglioni
Milan Fashion Week

Black
Pages: 34-35
Brand: Christian Dior
Season: Spring/Summer 2014
Creative Director: Raf Simons
Paris Fashion Week

White
Pages: 36-37
Brand: Stella McCartney
Season: Spring/Summer 2017
Creative Director: Stella McCartney
Paris Fashion Week

Grey
Pages: 38-39
Brand: Acne
Season: Autumn/Winter 2016
Creative Director: Jonny Johansson
Paris Fashion Week

Stripes
Pages: 40-41
Brand: Emporio Armani
Season: Autumn/Winter 2016
Creative Director: Giorgio Armani
Milan Fashion Week

Polka Dots
Pages: 42-43
Brand: Gucci
Season: Spring/Summer 2017
Creative Director: Alessandro Michele
Milan Fashion Week

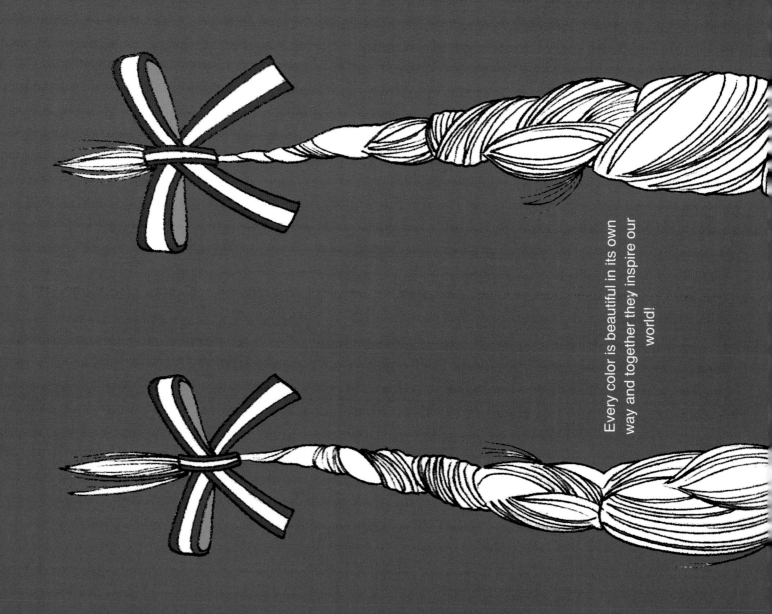

Every color is beautiful in its own way and together they inspire our world!

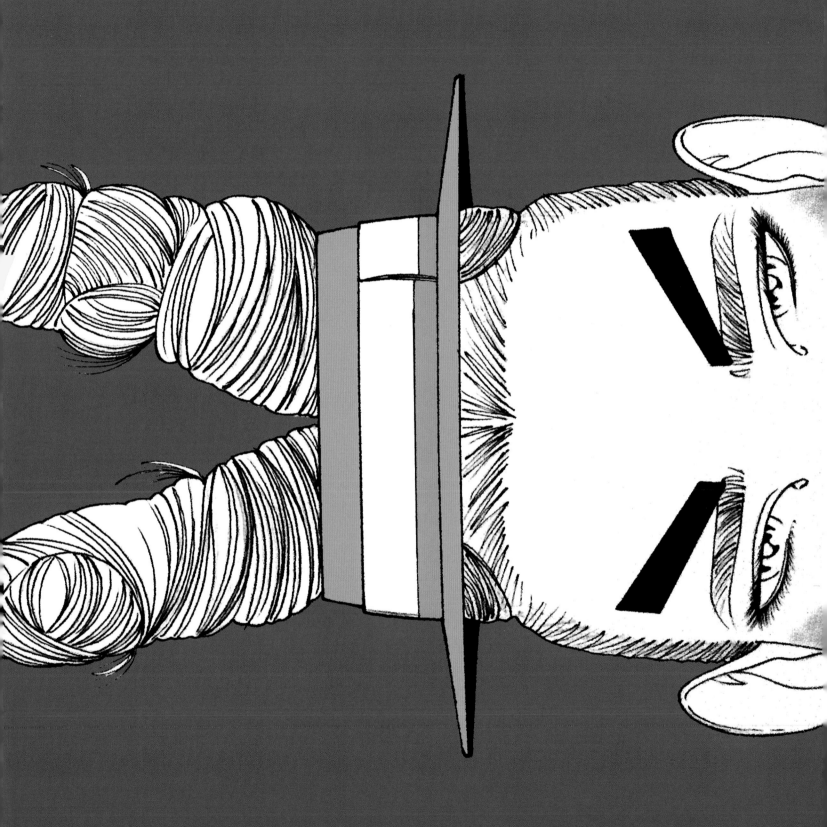

Clarence Ruth was born in New York in 1981. As a young
man in elementary school, he established success as an
artist by winning a number of first-place prizes in art
contests; one of those pieces was bought by JC Penney,
where it still hangs on the department store wall. Ruth's
artwork has also been displayed in museums. At a young
age Ruth decided to express his creativity through clothing
and began sketching out full collections. At that point Ruth
took fashion as his calling. After completing four years of
college in fashion design, Ruth established a successful
career as a fashion model and head of visuals for Andrew
Buckler, Ralph Lauren, Tom Ford, and GQ designer of the
year John Varvatos, to name a few. Ruth's work has been
seen throughout Manhattan and the Hamptons.